COOPER'S JOURNEY HOME

Elisabeth Copeland

Tampa, Florida

The content associated with this book is the sole work and responsibility of the author. Gatekeeper Press had no involvement in the generation of this content.

Cooper's Journey Home

Published by Gatekeeper Press
7853 Gunn Hwy., Suite 209
Tampa, FL 33626
www.GatekeeperPress.com

Copyright © 2024 by Elisabeth Copeland
All rights reserved. Neither this book, nor any parts within it may be sold or reproduced in any form or by any electronic or mechanical means, including information storage and retrieval systems, without permission in writing from the author. The only exception is by a reviewer, who may quote short excerpts in a review.

The editorial work for this book is entirely the product of the author. Gatekeeper Press did not participate in and is not responsible for any aspect of these elements.

No AI was used to generate any text in the manuscript.

Library of Congress Control Number: 2024933683

ISBN (paperback): 9781662949685
eISBN: 9781662949692

Thank you to our Houston community. Each of you made our journey a little less terrifying. Your support, gifts of comfort and your eagerness to provide for our family will forever be remembered.

Thank you to my husband, for your unconditional love.

Having experienced five failed pregnancies, I am no stranger to loss. There can be comfort in loss. Loss is safe. Final.

But this, the unknown we would have to battle together as a family every day for months? My heart was heavy with the overwhelming odds stacked against our premature infant.

You, our baby boy, were in for the fight of your life, and our family would fight along with you. Determined to bring you home.

Cooper Thomas, born February 15, 2021, 1 pound 10 ounces.

In your first week of life, I picked up a journal and began writing your story.

COOPER DAY 7

Hey, baby boy. You've made it one week so far. Your Dad and I have ridden an emotional roller coaster, but you are so damn worth it. To say we love you to the moon and back is an understatement. Tomorrow I will try to find the strength to write all you have overcome and achieved. Today I will say you have been strong and responsive to your care team's treatment plan. There are a dozen nurses and Neonatologists working toward your success. Dr. Singh just stopped by your room off his shift to check on you. He sat with me a while in the seating area at the back of our private room here at the Pavilion for Women hospital. That ambulance ride this morning did a number on your stats, and your vitals have been all over the place since we arrived this morning.

You are a little miracle, and your care team are each helping do what I couldn't. I'll only say this once, but I have to say it: I am so very sorry, my love, I could not have kept you warm longer.

To the moon, forever and always.
-Mom

COOPER DAY 8

Momma and Daddy can't both be with you today, or any day, due to COVID restrictions. Today is Dad's turn again so he is with you on this scary day. I am at home with Jordan and Grandma is sleeping. At noon the technicians will be taking a sonogram of your belly because the greyish-blue hue of your distended belly is not resolving on its own. I am slightly paralyzed with fear for the potential results. If you have a bowel obstruction, it means surgery. A surgery you would not survive. I am pausing my entry there until we know more.

You did not react well to the daily chest X-Ray this morning, so the sonogram has been postponed until tomorrow. My anxiety has been through the roof today. Dad said I should go on a walk and get some fresh air. As soon as Grandma wakes up from her nap, we will go check the mail.

Something AMAZING happened today. I called the NICU around noon in tears to beg for a COVID exception by testing negative daily because Dad and I so want to be there together with you. I feel helpless just sitting at home. The sweet Miss Annette who sits at the front desk of the unit, emotional herself with me on the phone, committed to update us when there was a change, but she unfortunately had previously had the same conversation with other parents too many times to count in the last year. It was out of our control. Well, not two hours later as Dad was leaving the NICU headed home Miss Annette stopped him to share the COVID restrictions have been lifted for all NICU parents. I cried, prayed, spoke my wish and need into the universe; manifestation of our dreams if only we are bold enough to speak them.

Remember that.

Love,
Mom

COOPER DAY 9

Baby steps today. Weaning down your oxygen support, from 100% to 90%. Neither level is sustainable for long. Your care plan for today is to continue to wean down and potentially move you from the Oscillator ventilator to the Jet ventilator. These two ventilator machines are the reason we moved you to this hospital. The Jet's level of support will still be hard on your lungs, but less so. You need time to grow and heal. Every move you make to a different level of support is expected to be gradual. Time may be what you need, we will not know until we try. You have an amazing team working to support you. You still prefer not to be messed with, and we limit touch times. We are taking notes of your personality already.

XOXO
-Mom

COOPER DAY 10

Most of the city is back to normal now. Where to even begin describing those first days of your life? During your first five days of life when we were at Houston Methodist, the entire hospital was on boil notice. I showered using bottled water. Not the post-delivery shower I had looked forward to enjoying. My breast pump parts had to be boiled after every pump, and with bottled water. The worry I carried about infecting you with dirty milk wore on me, like my nerves weren't already frazzled enough. Our OB came by your room on day two to check on us. She shared how hard it had been for the medical staff not to be able to travel home between shifts because of the road conditions. How difficult it was to scrub into surgery in a hospital with no running water. Superhumans. All of them.

Your second day of life was the end of your "honeymoon" period. Prior to your delivery, the NICU care team prepared us to expect a honeymoon period after birth if you could be saved with intubation. Your tiny body could handle living outside the womb with support for a few hours, or even a few days, but inevitably your underdeveloped bodily systems would tire out. And tired, they did. Your lungs began to show severe signs of distress. The Neonatologists said there were only two options – your body would give up, or you would need to be transported across town to the Houston Medical Center where they offered a higher level of support care. Being the problem solver I am, I even begged for the equipment to be moved to you. They patiently explained they did not have the training for the different machines.

Fair enough.

We could choose to wait for the transport a few more days, but if your situation became critical, your Neonatologist would make the transport call.

"HAVE YOU SEEN OUTSIDE?" Is what I wanted to scream when the word "transport" was uttered out loud. You had a head bleed, Grade 2, most likely from birth. The process is traumatic for tiny preemies who are not strong enough yet to travel through the birth canal. We could not touch you without your stats crashing and the suggestion, well, the only option presented, was: to move you from the bed you were currently in over to a transport isolette, to hook you up to all new monitors, to wheel you down the hall, down the elevator, then OUTSIDE through the ambulance bay, then to DRIVE 35 miles across partially frozen roads navigating insane drivers through the 4th most populated city in the United States to another large building with plenty of hallways and elevators to navigate before arriving at what would be your new home for, hopefully, months to come. I asked for other options and 'helicopter' was presented. We quickly moved back to discussing ambulance transport.

On day five of life, we could not wait any longer. As I parked my car at the hospital that morning I was speaking with two of my best friends who had called to check on us, letting them know that you had leveled back out the day prior. They asked over and over if I was ok. I could honestly say I was happy because you were alive. That was enough to keep me going. I took the elevator up to the fourth floor, signed in, scrubbed down and rolled in read to take on the day. By then this routine and this place felt familiar. Safe.

As I walked into the NICU, your care team was outside your door with grim faces. Even though morning doctor's rounds had not started yet they pulled me in and said we needed to talk. Overnight your body had begun shutting down and you swelled up like a seal. You stopped peeing, stopped taking fluids. This was it. It was time. You made the decision for us. We were calling for transport and your ride was on its way. For the next 45 minutes my head lay in my hands, doubled over crying in the corner chair next to your isolette. That was the first moment in your brief life that I thought you might not make it. In that moment, doubled over, carrying a crushing weight, completely defeated, I asked the nurse at least three times if she was certain your condition could not have been caused by dirty milk. If Dad or I somehow caused this when we reached our hands into your isolette. She assured me we did nothing wrong. "It was impressive he has made it as far as he has with the support available at the hospital, and this is what happens to tiny babies." I could not tell if she was just trying to make me feel better or not, but I decided I would have to give myself grace and move forward.

Within an hour the ambulance arrived. The process to move you to the transport isolette was no quick endeavor. The beeps of alarms caused by the disconnecting and connecting of sensors, leads, cuffs felt uncontrollable. Like when you drive without buckling your seatbelt. I cannot stand that noise. A sweet nurse I had connected with gently grabbed Dad and my hands and pulled us into the hall around the corner from your room. Close enough I could still hear the beeps, but also close enough to the outside window to feel the sun on my face. "Breathe in, breathe out." We laughed (a little) and shared stories. She did everything she could think of to distract us from what was happening ten feet away. Every few minutes I would stop mid-sentence and clue into the buzzing. Then they stopped.

You were packed up, and ready to roll. Only one parent could ride downtown with you in the ambulance. I hugged Dad good-bye, hopped up into the ambulance passenger seat and slowly the driver pulled away from the building. Our safety net. I had no idea what laid ahead for us. For you.

I don't handle the unknown well, and certainly not things out of my control. "Breathe in, breathe out" I told myself repeatedly. That was absolutely the longest 45 minutes of my life. With every tiny bump or turn my heart dropped to my stomach. Houston highways aren't the smoothest and the roads are basically Swiss cheese. I was shaky and I knew without a doubt that your head bleed we were incredibly concerned for did indeed worsen on that ride. How could it not?

The beeps from the transport isolette were different from the beeps and alarms from the NICU isolette you had lived in for your first five days. I was quickly trying to tune into which was a bad alarm and which was a really bad alarm based on the looks on the medical team's faces. All four of them were chatting away back there like we were waiting on our Starbucks orders. Alarms were ringing like the "Carol of the Bells" at Christmas.

We arrived at Texas Children's Pavilion for Women and took the ambulance entrance up. We wheeled into your room, but your room was not ready for us. "You have got to be fucking kidding me, this place is a shithole, get it together people. We have a sick kid here. My kid." almost leapt from my lips. Instead, I kept my mouth shut and smiled. You and your transport team had to wait in the hallway. I went for a walk to calm my nerves and get signed in. This was going to be home for a while, might as well get to know the place.

The first sweet face I met was the front desk receptionist- Miss Annette. Some people are blessed by God to be caretakers and her heart shone through in everything she did. Especially in that first conversation. She was patient, picked up on my mood and was gentle when offering information or managing expectations for the coming months. NICUs are secure, but even more so with COVID. The rules, the disappointing information that Jordan would never be able to visit, the extensive registration process required every day. It was all overwhelming and frustrating.

She toured me through the double doors just to her right first, the Ronald MacDonald family lounge. On the table were sandwiches donated from the deli downstairs. There were materials to properly label food placed in the community fridge. Oatmeal, hot chocolate, granola bars and coffee all out on the counter for everyone. A single flat screen TV with a few parents huddled around, and a gigantic window offering an awesome view of downtown.

On every drive I have taken through the Houston medical center I have looked up the stories of floors of each hospital and pondered the hundreds of reasons thousands of patients and visitors were inside the expansive buildings. A chemist researching medical treatments, or counselors offering end of life care. Nurses working long shifts for patients, some who would go home and others who would never feel the sun again.

At that moment I stood inside the building, realizing we were the family I had felt sorrow for before. I stepped up to the floor to ceiling window, looking down at traffic many stories below, wondering who was thinking of me. Of you. Of our family. The unknowns that lie before us. Who was driving through these streets, looking up, also not aware of what lies ahead for them?

Next, we went to the back of the unit, past dozens of shared and private NICU patient rooms, to the hallway alcove with the breast pump sanitizing station. A small space, 8'x6'. No door or curtain, but somewhat private. I couldn't imagine then I'd spend more than 70 hours inside that little alcove waiting for the microwave to sanitize my breast pump parts. Staring at the walls and blank cabinets as to give as much privacy as possible to the parents across the hall in their child's room. Mothers breastfeeding, doctors delivering confidential information. Though the halls were peaceful and welcoming, there was always an undertone of seriousness and restricted presence.

We journeyed past the nursing manager's office, milk bank drop-off, the communal showers and eventually back to you. Though there was some TCH (Texas Children's Hospital) red splashed throughout the unit, it was mostly sterile white with fluorescent lighting.

Within the hour, Dad had arrived. We could both be present in your room on intake day.

You struggled significantly on your first day at the new hospital. You were on the absolute highest lung support and your medical teams, day and night shift, emphasized that if your current level of respitory support did not keep you in safe ranges, there were no other options.

We understood, but that didn't make it any easier to hear. All we could do was pray and wait.

You could do this. I knew it.

XO
-Momma

COOPER DAY 11

We moved you to a different type of ventilator today - the Jet. You have been weaned off the daily insulin, dopamine (for BP and kidney support) and down to two hydrocortisone doses per day (Q12). So much progress! Your swelling looks a little better today and the greyish hue on your left side is improving. Love you so much, baby. I cannot ask any more from you right now. Your momma will always be patient with you and let you grow in your own time.

Promise.

XO

COOPER DAY 12

There was a time when we didn't know if you would have a day six... here we are day twelve! This journey is an emotional roller coaster, but Dad and I are settled in for the long haul. I will tell you for the rest of your life how thankful I am you are fighting and thriving to be here with us. You and I will be thick as thieves, and I can't wait to get to know you. To know your heart, the way you see the world. Our home is full of fun, "I love you" and joy. You are a lucky little boy, and we are so lucky to have you. I am about to leave the hospital and spend the afternoon with Jordan at the Children's Museum down the road. All he knows is "Cooper sleeps at a different house right now." He can't wait to meet you. We cannot wait to have you there. For my heart to feel whole. How can a mother feel whole when her family sleeps under different roofs?

'BTW - you haven't started eating again yet, but I have two gallons of milk waiting for you.

XOXO
- Momma

COOPER DAY 14

Hey, love! What a day! I was able to change your diaper for the first time. Until now, I've mostly had gentle finger tip touches to your skin. Today feeling how thin and sticky your skin is to the touch, expecially around your vital organs, is a bit unnerving. You are so small and precious. Also, today I saw your right eye begin to open just a sliver. My heart absolutely BURST! Dad was working this morning, so I called him and sent a video of your first blinks. We cannot wait to hold you, baby boy. Over the last 48 hours you've made big ventilator changes and are weaning off NO (Nitric Oxide) today. You've done great so far! We are scheduled to receive an updated head ultrasound report tomorrow. If ever there was a prayer to be answered it would be for your brain bleed to have improved since last week. No matter what, our love for you is only growing. Whatever the report shows, we will deal with it together.

-Momma-

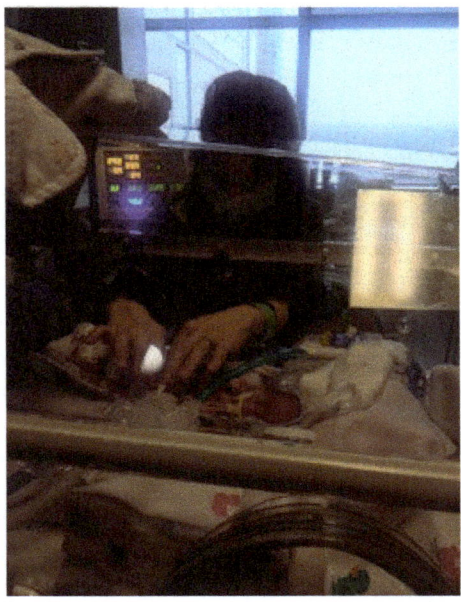

COOPER DAY 15

March 1

Today has been a weird day. So many ups and downs, just since I arrived at 8:15am. I have been here every morning for rounds since you were born (except for the two days Dad was here and I couldn't be due to COVID rules.) We weaned you off Nitric Oxide and are working to wean down sedatives-Fentanyl and something else I always forget. Your Jet/vent settings are relatively low. Today has been an adjustment day for you. We did a follow-up head ultrasound and I'm waiting to go over the results with your Neonatologist Dr. Gupta. I grabbed lunch from the downstairs cafeteria. After I finished, I came right back upstairs and walked into your room to your care team trying to fix your stats. I heard the commotion before I saw it.

With your alarms firing loudly, the nurse shouted down the hall for a Respitory Therapist (RT). She shot up the top of your isolette bed with the push of a button and bagged you. She gently placed a tiny facemask over your nose and mouth with a pint sized balloon in her palm and squeezed, manually pushing air in and out of your lungs, though all I've heard for weeks is that you need the ventilator to survive and prevent your lungs from collapsing. There have been little moments that have caught me off guard already, that for only a second the thoughts occur, "Is this the issue you can't overcome? Is this the problem your team cannot solve for you? Is this the thing that kills you?" All I want is for you to be ok and comfortable. All we can ask of you is to keep breathing and growing. After a walk around the entire unit, I returned to a calm room. The RT was able to adjust your tubes and your stats leveled back out. No more screaming alarms.

Today you would have you would have been 26 weeks & 4 days gestation. This morning during doctor rounds your Fellow, Neonatologist and nurse all said you are exceeding expectations.

That does bring comfort. I don't get the vibe from these professionals they give out false hope.

You are such a joy already and have so many people across twelve states praying for you and cheering you on. I might post your first Instagram post today or tomorrow if I have the energy. We want to share your journey, but it feels daunting. Not certain how to explain the experience. Your experience.

The nurse who yelled down the hall for help, threw up the top of your isolette and bagged you was a freaking rock star. She was cool, calm, methodical, and as I got up to leave, she was able to simultaneously reassure me and urge me to stay because she had this under control. When I came back, I told her how much I appreciated her and how impressed I was. I sure hope she heard that. Because she is the kind of nurse that should be at the bedside of the sick children with their families. These nurses don't just care for the child, they care for the whole team.

We were asked by a doctor who previously had been director of the unit to participate in a NEC (Necrotizing Enterocolitis) study. I said "Please sign us up" before he could finish explaining. He said usually families want to research the study and understand why samples were being collected. I was excited to share and be a part of any research that helped more babies. All participation in this study required was taking your stool and urine samples periodically working to identify leading indicators of NEC before an infection developed. It can be devastating for a preemie. We met quite a few parents who were fighting the NEC battle, among other things, in the NICU.

Of all the battles you are facing, they all fall in the normal 'to be expected from a 2lb human' range. So far, we've been lucky. Keep it up, kid!

Love,
Momma

COOPER DAY 16

1lb, 13oz!!!

Major gains! You've gained 3 ounces since birth. Jordan knows Daddy goes to the gym to get muscles and boy you've got this gains thing down. You're eating momma's milk again! Tolerating small feeds every three hours (2mL's). There may come another day while in the NICU you don't eat, and we are prepared for another step backwards. But if you could just keep this up, we'd really appreciate it.

Great news- your head bleed is healing! For years I've fought hard to not sweat the things I cannot control. Your growth, development, tolerance to changes in your environment, how well you transition to the regular ventilator from the Jet ventilator (in 15 minutes! Eek!) are all things I can't control and that you will do in your own time. How your body reabsorbs your head bleed and how quickly your brain recovers is high on my list of worries, but highest on the list of things I cannot control. I love you, Cooper. I love your heart, your willingness to thrive in a world you weren't ready for and your fighting spirit when the fight in me wasn't enough. To be fair, my body gave up, not my heart.

What you have already overcome:

- Premature birth – ruptured membranes
- Birth at 24 weeks, 3 days
- Four doses of surfactant
- Intubation at birth
- Began feeds at day two, but digestion shut down day five
- Renal failure, no kidney output for 24 hours
- No poop for eight days
- Abdominal edema (technically it's edema everywhere, but the belly swelling is most pronounced and causing concern)
- Discoloration

- Scared for a bowel perforation, but were unable to diagnose
- Grade 2 head bleed (diagnosed Day 4)
- Grade 3/4 head bleed (Diagnosed Day 8)
- Unbalanced electrolytes

Currently on:

- Fentanyl (pain and anesthesia)
- Versed (sedative)
- Dopamine (BP & Renal)
- Insulin (your levels were up to 370, where normal is 70 – 100)
- Steroids (multiple, I believe 3 rounds, but it may have been 4)
- Sodium acetate (reduce blood gasses)
- Antibiotics (second week of life)
- Caffeine (every morning)
- Standard ventilator day 1-5 ($FIO_2$3 40%-50%)
- Oscillator Day 5-13 (FIO_2 90%-100%)
- Jet Day 13 – TBD
- Six blood transfusions and counting
- Lasix (diuretic needed now that you're back on momma's milk)

Lil'gansta. Keep rollin'!

XO
-Momma

COOPER DAY 17

1lb, 12.2oz

Man, today did not start out as planned. Dad fell to the ground at home from a back spasm while getting Jordan dressed and yelled for me from across the house. Poor Jordan was so worried for Dad. I didn't know how to help him, and I was anxious to beat morning traffic to arrive at the hospital for your doctors' rounds. We were able to get Dad walking around and to the couch, and our neighbor is checking on him later this morning. Felt awful needing to be in two places at the same time to help everyone.

We are starting you on steroids today. It's your 4th round. The standard of care for steroid use is usually only three rounds. Based on a few of your stats, we were told the pros outweigh the cons and your Neonatologist recommends the 4th dose. When I expressed my concern for the additional dose after previous extensive conversations around the standard three, your doctor offered me the choice. "Um, what? Pardon me?" As of today, I am officially a member of your care team. I am feeling simultaneously overwhelmed and empowered. Since this is a different type of steroid aimed at reducing inflammation in your lungs, I told your doctor I was on board to move forward with his plan. Eeeek.

If successful, we may move you to CPAP this week and remove the intubation tube. About 11am today Dad was able walk, drive and get to the chiropractor for an adjustment. Our bodies have taken a beating these last few months as much as our souls have these last few weeks. Once you come home, we are all going on vacation. Your Dad and I cannot wait to have our boys under the same roof. I also can't wait to hear your first cry.

XOXO
-Momma-

COOPER DAY 18

Tell me how cool this is! Part of your lung immaturity is the reduced capacity to turn over oxygen to carbon dioxide AND eliminate it from your system. Your ABG (blood gas level tested by taking blood samples) is checked Q12 (twice a day) to determine if you're still in normal range or close to acidotic (too much carbon dioxide building up in your system). We removed your arterial line yesterday, so now it's all heel pricks for blood samples. I don't like that because more holes punctured into your tiny body are more opportunities for infection. But they assure me it's less risk of infection than keeping the arterial line in place. I'm sorry, baby. During morning rounds reviewing your stats from this morning's heel prick, the Neonatologist pointed to your fluctuating chloride/phosphorus and noted your metabolic system is attempting to compensate where your respiratory system is exhausted. Wow. The human body is beyond intelligent. Sodium chloride was added to your TPN to facilitate the conversion. When one tired bodily system borrows resources from another, that system will eventually exhaust, too. Trying to get ahead of that and get you back in balance. Tomorrow we'll see if it worked.

Cooper, I realized on my way home from the hospital today that one day you will read these pages. You will grow, learn to crawl, walk, talk and then to read. Oh, how you will love to read. To learn. I'll make certain of it. Two of your grandparents were teachers. They'll make certain of it, too. I'll try my best here to capture your first day of life. The journey to the hospital and eventually your very scary arrival. When you are old enough to read these pages, ask me questions. Ask me to tell you the story over and over again. Let us together never lose sight of the miracle.

At 1:00 am in the morning of February 15, 2021, I woke Dad. The cramps I felt were well beyond normal pregnancy discomfort. I had been directed to at home bed rest for three weeks after

placing a second rescue cerclage stitch at 20 weeks gestation, a last attempt to save your pregnancy as long as possible. Until that morning, bed rest had been smooth sailing physically. Mentally I was a mess. But that morning something was different. Something was not right, and if what I feared was truly happening, best case scenario we only had hours to make it to the hospital. Even though my gut told me I was not in labor, we needed help.
One of the worst winter storms in Texas history had struck the night prior and continued to swirl outside- Winter Storm Uri. Record lows ushered in sleet and snow, causing road closures, power outages, and broken watermains. Our average twenty-five-minute drive to our hospital was covered in half an inch of ice and layers of snow. Texans do not own the proper tires or have the experience driving in those conditions. Your poor father. The pressure he felt that evening making that journey I hope he never has to experience again.

We had been here together before. Dad and I had rushed to the ER in 2019, a few weeks after my cerclage was placed with Jordan, because I was bleeding in the middle of the night. That had been terrifying enough, but the roads had been completely passable. The pains I experienced that evening with Jordan felt like pelvic growing pains, normal for many pregnancies, and I brushed them off. As the night progressed so did the level of pain and eventually my brain told me to get up and move around. As soon as I stood, blood gushed, and I panicked. Dad threw together a hospital bag for both of us, helped me up into the truck and rushed us down the streets to the hospital at 3:00 am. In the years we have been together, your Dad has proven to be the most reliable figure in my life. He is a rock. My rock.
Turned out it was nothing major that night with Jordan and I was sent home to rest. Poor Dad had curled himself into the fetal position, trying to sleep in two uncomfortable metal-framed chairs in the emergency room. He does the most with the least when he must, and I love him for it.

This time with you was different. Winter Storm Uri changed everything. The city was shut down, and the ambulance would not come to get us. Let me clarify: the ambulance would not come to get us and take us where we needed to go. I called 911 and after our call for transport was initially refused by dispatch, I asked for the ambulance dispatch directly. He said he could come get us but, two things he said had me fuming in a silent rage. I could not believe what I was hearing. 1) The ambulance crew would need to drive very slowly, so it would be a while. 2) They were under emergency protocols and limited to transporting us to the nearest hospital.

The closest hospital was not an option because the hospital four miles from our home was a regional hospital with no NICU. "What if we make it half-way there on our own and we slide into the ditch, then I call again?" I attempted to negotiate. "Then ma'am, we'll pick you up and slowly take you to the nearest hospital." There was nothing we could do.

We had to attempt it on our own.

Our good friend and sweet neighbor walked over in the snow to stay at our home with Jordan, leaving her son and her husband home in the cold and the dark. Dad helped me up into the truck and off we went. Luckily, we parked in the garage and did not need to defrost the windshield. From the look of our neighbor's vehicles, we would have been severely delayed. Heat on full blast and the defrost pounding out some serious air, it was loud inside the truck. Outside the vehicle, a vastly different scene. No streetlamps illuminated our path, blinking red lights flashed where stoplights typically signaled due to the power outage. I only remember passing four or five vehicles on our drive, and each traveling as cautiously as we were that morning. Honestly, I asked Dad to speed up due to the terror I felt we would not make it in time. We were tense but quiet. I prayed every moment of that drive, my heart dropping to my toes every time the tires slipped on the ice. My hands on my stomach. Dad's hands tightly gripping the wheel. The snow was still flurrying, but not enough to prevent a view from the front windshield. We could see far enough in front of us to avoid a collision and attempt to stay out of the ditch. The emptiness of the dark night beyond our truck foreboded the dark uncertainty that lied ahead at the hospital.

We sled down the road for 40 minutes, but we made it safely. Dad dropped me at the entrance to the emergency room, then went to park the truck. I was still in a mild state of panic. Waddling through the automatic doors into the brightly lit entrance of the hospital, the all-too familiar temporary security desk consisting of a folding table, box of masks, and hand sanitizer was set up just to the right and the single night security guard's only gesture was to raise his arm and point me in the direction I needed to continue to find the front desk. Everyone I encountered believed immediately in my request for help because no one in their right mind would have come to the hospital unless in a true emergency. Their quick action to support me, taking my information while helping me into a wheelchair made the experience a tad less petrifying.

They sent me upstairs to the maternity ER floor. Within thirty minutes and after a few tests, we discovered that yes, my water had broken and yes, I was in labor. Your pregnancy was twenty-three weeks and three days along. I pushed down the thoughts clawing their way into my mind, trying to drown me in fear. As deep down as I could. Everything would be okay. This child would live.

The on-call doctor ordered magnesium to stop my labor. I received the first of two steroid shots deep in my ass to help stimulate your lungs in case you arrived. Those needles deliver a special kind of pain. Felt like it stabbed my bone. Antibiotics were also started in my IV because we did not know how long your fluid membranes had been ruptured. Infection can set in rapidly.

The nurse ordered a standard COVID test. Even though I knew I did not have it, I panicked again. Would they treat me like a leper during my own delivery if the test popped back positive? My rational mind knew I didn't have the virus because we had been physically quarantined at home and I was asymptomatic. Still, I sweated through those fifteen minutes. The test came back negative, but my heart goes out to all the mommas during the COVID years who had to be quarantined. Delivering a baby during a pandemic is highly unrecommended.

Over the next three hours, while the world outside froze, the magnesium drip continued to flow. Hot flashes and brain fog overwhelmed me. I attempted to communicate to my doctor and the nurse that I felt you were trying to make your debut. The pressure in my pelvis was all too familiar. But neither my doctor, nor my nurse, could understand what I was saying. My tongue weighed 5 pounds and the brain pulses I attempted to send to my mouth were delayed by several seconds. I was trapped inside my own body, helpless to share my feelings and fear. That magnesium was a bitch. The inability to communicate was excruciating, especially since it was such an important piece of information I needed someone to hear. Something of what I tried to share must have gotten through. The doctor did a quick evaluation and realized you were about to arrive.

Given the state of the weather and the hurried nature in which we had left the house, Dad had gone back home to check on Jordan and pack him a bag. Our wonderful neighbors (we then lived in the best cul de sac in Texas!) let Jordan bounce back and forth between their homes amidst the power outage and freezing temperatures, all while taking care of their own children during the first three days we were at the hospital. As close as we were to many of our neighbors before that night, the bonds we formed during this experience and the coming weeks have forever joined our hearts to the wonderful friends we call family. He hugged Jordan good-bye and headed back to the hospital.

All signs pointed to your arrival being eminent. The room was prepared your delivery. If I remember correctly, there were at least 12 people in our room. I moved into position and our doctor's kind words braced us for what was next. The magnesium drip intended to slow labor had been disconnected from my IV, and a different type of pain was setting into my body. Over the course of what couldn't have been more than 10 minutes the contractions were coming back on hard. Two big contractions came. Halfway through the third contraction, your heart rate dropped. The doctor told me to push. I pushed. HARD. You were born weighing 1 pound, 10.5 ounces.

During a standard delivery there is a lot of commotion in the delivery room. Add to that the extra hands on your team who were there to make sure you were stable and could be intubated. Dad held my hand and looked at me silently. We knew we each had the same questions loudly marching across our minds. "Were you stable?", "Could you breathe?", "Would we be able to catch a glimpse of you before they wheeled you to the NICU?"

While most of the room focused their attention on you, my doctor began sewing me up. Since I had no epidural, I could feel everything. Because you came so quickly, my body didn't have time to get warmed up. My cervix and vaginal wall were still tight, so even though you were small, I tore in three places internally.

Ouch.

"You don't have to hurt for this," my doctor offered graciously. "We can get you to the OR, get a spinal block, and finish." We agreed, and she packed the tears with gauze, so I didn't bleed out. It felt like she stuffed me with an entire dry beach towel. There was so much pressure, it took a moment to catch my breath.

Within minutes the nurses had already called for anesthesia and booked an operating room. We waited for the green light and for anesthesia to come clear me. I asked repeatedly, "Is he still ok? Is he still breathing?" The answer was always, "Yes, he's doing great."

That was the best we could hope for in that moment, so I wasn't panicked, or even scared. If a preemie of that size can be successfully intubated and oxygenate their body, then the additional life support that can be offered has a chance at sustaining life. From that moment and for the next days and weeks, I would smile and tell myself, "At least he's alive!"

Both Dad and I took a moment alone to process what had just happened. I stared silently at the ceiling. Dad sat down on the couch next to me, his head dropped in his hands, and our sweet doctor stood with him for a moment rubbing his back. As more moments passed, her face morphed from sympathetic to business to angst. At one point she announced to the room, "We need to get her in there so she doesn't bleed out".

That was the first moment of realization for me that what had been bad for all of us could still get worse. The anesthesiologist came to my bedside and asked the standard questions, "Do you understand the risks?" "What is your name?" Questions I did not feel we really had the time for, but I digress. The nurses quickly rolled me down the hall to the OR, the spinal block was placed, and within minutes, my doctor finished her stitching.

That was that. You were here. The turmoil of worry over how much longer I could hold you in was over. The rest was up to you.

COOPER DAY 19

My eyes swell with water every time I leave your brother and every time I leave you. Wanting to be in two places at once, 30 miles and 45 minutes apart wears on my soul. Today, the nurse has listed your patient goals as the following:
- Wean fentanyl
- Decrease Oxygen requirements
- Increase feeds and grow

Over the last three days, since weaning off NO and off the Jet to the Ventilator, your lungs have been a bit cloudier. But you are holding steady around 35%-40% FIO2. We are checking ABG Q12 and chest x-rays daily to determine if the new round of steroids are working (10 days tapered beginning Day 17). Dr. Singh noted we should see improvements within the first 3-4 days. This will be day three, so we'll see!

While at the hospital yesterday afternoon your Grandpa Dale called to let us know Great Grandpa Roy passed. Grandpa Dale and Great Uncle Dave have spent the last many months traveling up to New York to stay with him and make sure he was cared for with his failing health. He was a funny man with a twisted sense of humor. He always had everyone laughing even at the end of his long and beautiful life. Your Dad wishes he could fly up to be with our family, but he does not want to leave you. Even though our hearts are torn, please always know you and Jordan will be our first priority.

Love,
Mom and Dad

Ok, there's more for today:
Talking with my Hand to Hold mentor on the way home from the hospital (Katy, love her!) and she said something that resonated

with me. I said I was all over the place today as your care team considers extubating you. She reminded me it is terribly uncomfortable pulling back support at any stage. Her reply "It makes so much sense to feel what you're feeling. It would be odd to feel normal." Ain't that the truth of all truths? For fucks sake nothing about this is normal. I completed a leadership training course last semester at Rice and have begun Development Coaching. The training drove home for me that while I typically enjoy the uncomfortable space where growth occurs, not everyone does. Growth and progress happen in uncomfortable spaces and your only job right now is growth. Makes sense to be uncomfortable. Momma doesn't like that for you, but it's high on the list of things I do not have control over. Keep up the hard work!

COOPER DAY 20

Thank you!

To the neonatologists who problem solved, took the time to understand you and pushed you towards independence every step of the way.

To the Respiratory Therapists who rushed to your side when you needed it, participated in the care team's plan, and spent time with the nurses to train and troubleshoot.

To the nutritionists who ensured your care team's recommendations for TPN mix made sense for you every day those first many weeks.

To the infectious disease team who closely monitored your leg sore from birth and ongoing care of your many lines.

To the nurses, your advocates when I wasn't around or when you needed a change. Thank you for loving on our boy.

To Hand to Hold, thank you for your immediate response and pairing with my mentor. Experiencing this journey alongside my mentor and knowing her little boy did all the hard things, too made our journey not so scary.

To the receptionist team at the NICU who made every visit safe and special.

To the Kangaroo Kare transport team who moved us across Houston safely. Melody, N.P., who came with us to ensure you were stable!

To the pastoral care team that sat and listened.

To the COVID care lobby reception team at TCH who grew to know Dad and me.

To the sanitation team that kept your room clean. I watched when they came in daily, and they did a superb job.

To the friends and family care team following our progress and ensuring the best care.

To the Methodist West Team @ the NICU that cared the best they could for you and quickly identified when your care needs exceeded their resources.

To the Special Children's Rodeo Committee. I have called you friends for eight years, and now I call some of you family. Your support during this time meant the world.

To the Baker Hughes Houston team supporting my husband and our family- your gift for parking and transportation help made a big impact.

Thank you to ESG, for giving me as much space, support and time as I needed while knowing my job was secure and waiting for me when the time was right. What a blessing and relief from stress.

'Thank you to our families. No one lives near us, yet they have each done what they can to cover us in love and support as best they could. Vists, meals delivered. Gifts sent for Jordan. Thank you, from the bottom of our hearts. We love you.

COOPER DAY 21

It's 11am and it's quiet. Never quiet for long around here. But those quiet moments when your vitals look great, you're comfortable or sleeping bring so much peace to my heart. The alarms (either yours or someone else's) fire off every few minutes. I read a nurse's computer screen saver yesterday and it listed signs of alarm fatigue. It's real and I feel it. You love laying on your belly. Your knee and your nose are a little red from laying in your favorite position, so the nurse switched you to nose prongs for a few hours and then switched you back to a mask with extra cushion. While you had the prongs inserted, I noticed a tiny dimple at the end of your nose. A birth mark, or a scar? We'll see!

Every time there is a change in your support machines or tubes, the alarm beeps feel uncontrollable. The tight anxiousness I feel in my body is uncomfortable. I'm sure you're uncomfortable, too. Your eyes are a little smushed and it makes me sad, but your little face would have been smushed in-utero, too. So, I'll just have to deal and wait for you to grow and heal.

No matter the frustration, beeps, or the uncomfortable moments, nothing can compare to the fact that you OPENED YOUR EYES TODAY!

XOXO
-Momma

COOPER DAY 22

Today is a hard day for me. Your belly is distended again. This time it is most likely gas/air being pushed in by the CPAP and not an infection. It breaks my heart to see you uncomfortable. If holding you was the answer, I'd never put you down. The plan is to move you to a different ventilator, the bubble ventilator, today and increase your feed volumes. We'll hopefully see a change by tomorrow.

Please, God.
XOXO
-Mom

COOPER DAY 23

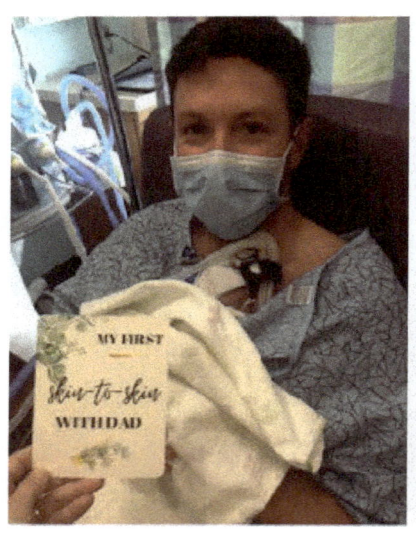
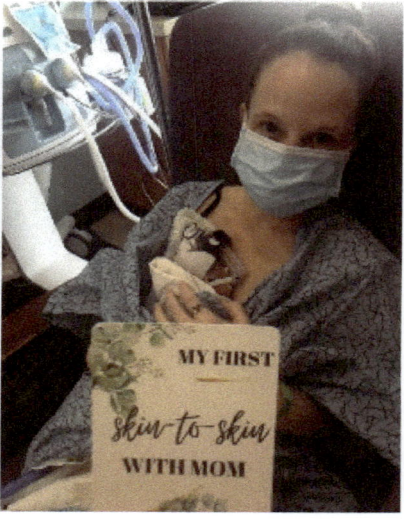

COOPER DAY 24

To pass the time, I read. A lot. I love reading but it's not something I've made time for these last few years. My favorite book I read in our time here at the NICU is now one of my favorite stories of all time. *Running with Sherman* by Christopher McDougall. Chris finds Sherman, a rescue donkey on the brink of death and seemingly hopeless. He decides to save Sherman but doesn't know the first thing about donkeys. The parallels to saving Sherman and saving you resonated with me every day I picked up the pages: the power of the human spirit, the spirit of all living things' innate desire to live.

COOPER DAY 26

Let me tell you about a little hidden gem – Pine Forest Country Club. Dad and I joined the spring after we married. We loved golfing together 3-4 times a week and met some of the most amazing people there. As soon as I went on bedrest with you, we decided to quit the club. Many friends were sad to see us go, but we knew the great friends we'd met would be around long after our membership expired. And boy, were we right! This morning some friends came by to drop off a check, a big check, from friends that wanted our family to be able to focus on you. You're loved, kid. Remember always that God puts the right people in your life at the right time. One day you will be the right person for someone else and you'll be able to pay it forward.

XOXO
-Momma

(Dad)

Cooper,

Today has just been one of those days that makes you feel blessed. This morning we had some friends of ours drop off a very generous gift in your name. You are so loved, kiddo. Everyone who knows our family has expressed their love for you in many ways. We are at the hospital now, sitting right beside you. Mom just got done with some skin-to-skin time. We cannot express how good it feels to hold you, Cooper. We love you so very much. Proud of you.

You've started making these baby "coo" sounds and it just warms our hearts when we hear them. We are by your side, every step of the way, son.

Love you,
Dad

COOPER DAY 27

For my NICU library, I brought a book from home with me. Hoda Kotb's *I Really Needed This Today*. I read it every single morning. Some days the message was a breath of fresh positivity, and other days it's like God wrote it himself for me.

Hoda's message today was "A lot of beautiful things can happen if only you believe." This week has been amazing. Stats have been more stable. You're moving a little more often, looks like you're trying to get comfortable.

Our skin to skin was stressful for me today, though I did get to hold you for the entire three hours. That has been a rare occurrence to date. I really had to pee from the moment you were laid into my arms.

You were so relaxed. Your mouth would not stay shut, letting the oxygen being pushed in your nose escape. With the air escaping your mouth and not making it to your lungs, your O2 dropped constantly and the dreaded beeping about sent me over the edge. I had to hold your mouth closed for an hour and a half with my wrist all twisted, when all I wanted to do was hold your hand. My fingers began to fall asleep and tingle, and all I could do was wait it out. Extreme discomfort on my part, but you were sleeping peacefully.

This is parenting.

XOXO
-Momma

COOPER DAY 33

2lbs, 2.9oz

Do you even know how much we are falling in love with you? Looking at you today just compared to yesterday you look thicker and stronger. You are still fluid restricted because of your PDA (abnormal flow of the blood in the heart, often due to prematurity) & lungs, but you are growing at the rate we want you to be. Keep it up!

Today for the first time I felt as though I'm along this ride with you, not just waiting for you. Something inside me has changed and the energy I feel around this experience has changed, too. The pendulum swung!

COOPER DAY 35

Quiet day around here. I've already taken five walking laps around the unit. Walking slow enough to peak in each room at the little ones but not long enough to make any families uncomfortable. Sitting in your room feels isolating. It helps me to see the other parents here. All with lives outside these walls but for now here is where we need to be. I counted 42 rooms in total, but some rooms hold more than one baby at a time. Unreal to know this many little lives started too soon.

Cooper. I love the name we chose for you. Sounds like you'll be an athlete. We would be ok if you wanted to dance, become an astronomer or love drawing comics, too. Up to you, love. Here is the story of how I chose your name.

Dad and I had gone back and forth on a name for months. We narrowed our favorites down to Austin or Cooper. When I was on bedrest, the OB determined a second rescue cerclage stitch was needed and it became an emergent prodecure. We rushed to the hospital. The anesthesiologist came into the pre-op prep room to run through the surgery sign-off with me while dad signed in down the hall. When he introduced himself as Dr. Cooper, tears began to stream down both sides of my face as I laid there on the bed. He turned up one eyebrow in a look of curiosity.

Through the tears, half-smiling, I asked if I could explain the tears, he nodded. I shared we had been toggling back and forth on choosing a name and my pregnant, hormonal brain in that moment decided my baby boy would live and his name would be Cooper. He offered a tender grin. I am fairly certain his look conveyed that moment did not change his life, but it certainly changed mine.

COOPER DAY 36

It is beautiful outside today. The view of the medical center and the Houston Galleria from your 10th floor room is just what the doctor ordered. I can't wait for you to go outside and feel the sun. Maybe we can find you baby sunglasses your size. Dad always finds the coolest baby accessories.

Your oxygen levels continue to swing like Tarzan, but you are growing, eating, and sleeping most of the day. You're doing great, baby! We can't wait to get you home!

XOXO
-Mom

(Dad)
As our routines changed while you were in NICU, we tried to find ways to help us get through the day by finding activities we both enjoyed. We would listen to audio books to and from the hospital, especially on Fridays when we went together. We tried to think of something other than the obstacles you would have to endure before coming home. One of those was the book, *Glass Castle*. A memoir about the details of a woman's upbringing and dysfunctional family. We would laugh with each other and be thankful that we didn't have it as bad. Even with you in the hospital, it was nowhere near as bad as what she went through. It made us feel blessed in a way, knowing that we are a loving family, who also have extended family loving and supporting us. Even though times were tough, things could have ended up being way worse. We'd also make time for just the two of us to grab a late lunch and a beer at a local brewery on the way home from the hospital. We tried to do it on Fridays before going to pick up Jordan from school. Just another way for the two of us to spend a little time together, reminding ourselves that we will always be there for each other, and that we were blessed.

COOPER DAY 37

I've been here an hour and a half, and you've had four Brady alarms already. Much more frequent than the last few days. Breaks my heart, but you could also just be working on a big poop. Bearing down and holding your breath can have the same effect as a cardiac event, as far as the monitors are concerned.

Spoke to Dr. Hancock this morning about your lung development and treatments. He connected some dots for me today: the goal is to grow, because growth brings new healthy lung tissue not previously damaged by the Oscillator, Jet or ventilator. Previously damaged lung tissue will not repair itself. Only new lung growth will take you home safely. You still need support, but just enough support to foster new growth while avoiding damaging any new lung growth. The key is to find the right balance, which changes every day.

Yeesh.

He also highly recommended to begin reading to you aloud. Babies who are read to thrive at higher rates than those who are not. It isn't a cure-all but it is important. So read, we will. We read to Jordan every day. For whatever reason, honestly, the thought of reading to you had not crossed my mind. For weeks we tried to leave you alone. Minimal stimulation was a requirement for everyone on your care team.

How could I have not thought about reading to you? With a degree in Child Development, it should have been first on my list. I envision so many activities with you once you are home. But not here. I don't feel in control here. These are not the plans I have for you. Having not thought of reading to you makes me feel like a bad mom. It shows me how far I still must go before I truly see you as whole. As a baby. As my son.

You are really starting to grow, keep it up please! Every day you grow is one step closer to coming home. We love your little face so much and cannot wait to wake up with you on Saturday mornings watching cartoons and cuddling with your big brother.

Come home to us!!
XO
-Mom

COOPER DAY 38

March 24

Today during our cuddle time your neighbor friend needed the crash cart. Outside in the hallway it looked and sounded like everyone in the unit came to support our hallway of tiny babies, and you, because your nurse was needed next door. What an emotional experience for everyone. The baby recovered quickly, but it's a heavy reminder every moment is precious.

We have a routine now: I hold you for your noon feeding, after one hour you flip your head and the obnoxious mask and hose covering your faces flips, too. After two hours you get antsy and want back in your isolette. Then you have a massive poop! The nurse even asked if I wanted to change your diaper today after our hold time. I am certain it's because she knew what was coming when I put you back into your bed. I love you, baby boy. See you again for our date tomorrow.

Love,
Momma

REFLECTING ON NICU DAY 39

The entry I never wrote but will never forget was the one for the next day. Dad and I were there together as we were most Fridays. I was holding you at noon again and not five minutes into your feed we heard hurried steps running down the hall in the opposite direction as the day prior. The baby on the other side of us who was just a few weeks younger than you (born around the same 24-week gestation) needed help.

Upon admittance to the Pavilion NICU we were told that your room becomes an operating room (OR) in critical situations. One of the many reasons for the level of cleanliness required- no food or open drink containers, constant sanitization. It was extremely rare that a super preemie would be moved for any reason.

As the hurried feet in the hallway became louder, we saw two or three Respiratory Therapists (RT) and a few nurses pass by in the hall. Then another Neonatologist, whizzing left to right one after another across our doorway. Then more people we didn't recognize in OR gear. Dad met my gaze from across the room. Our hearts dropped. After many minutes an entire team was in front of your doorway, her isolette being slowly wheeled down the hall in front of our room.

Not 90 seconds later the entire team came back slowly down the hall, past your doorway in the opposite direction, and wheeled her back into her room. The parents were just outside our door. I so wanted to run and embrace that mom swimming in a sea of tears. She was beside herself. A nurse popped open the storeroom closet across from your room and allowed her and her husband a private, sheltered moment in there away from the chaos.

The thoughts that crept across my mind in those moments were: "I couldn't imagine you being so sick that we had to wheel you down toward the operating room. And then to immediately realize you're too sick for even that so let's just wheel you back." When they say that the NICU is a roller coaster, this is the type of situation to which they are referring. We learned later that she needed to be intubated but her esophagus was slightly snaked. Her team of doctors and RTs were troubleshooting the best they could while being as careful as possible not to perforate. These people really are miracle workers. Someone was able to finally apply the right touch, get the tube in and she was steady again. A week or two later we saw the parents in the break room, introduced ourselves and we've been friends ever since. There's something about this place that bonds you in the best way amidst the worst of circumstances.

The next Monday we met with your team during rounds, and they asked if we were ready to move across the unit to the big baby hall. We were graduating from the micro-preemie hall. A nurse said, "Cooper isn't the sickest baby anymore and another baby needs this room."

COOPER DAY 42

March 28

Lucas was born last night. A tiny preemie also needing lots of support to breathe on his own. I hope by the time you read this we still know Lucas and his family, and you are friends with sweet Lucas. His mom and I have both had such difficult journeys becoming moms. You will both have amazing stories to tell.

When I walked into your room this morning, I was ELATED to find your oxygen FIO2 was down to 29.7%. We haven't seen a number in the 20's in a long time. You gained 3oz in the last three days, but some is just fluid weight. Hopefully holding you today helps move and drain some of your retained fluid. The nurse has begun a little daily fluid massage around your face where the facemask lays. After care times this afternoon, the Respiratory Therapist showed us how do to it ourselves. You always look a little less puffy after.

Love you, baby.
-Momma

COOPER DAY 47

April 2

Man, you are rocking and rolling. I held you for two hours today with your noon feeding. It is Granny Di's birthday today, so I have to make it home for a birthday dinner. The first 30 minutes of our cuddle time you hardly bubbled and never de-satted. These are great signs your lung reserves are increasing and maturing. It's not a race to the finish line. Growth happens on the journey. It's still a long journey home. Don't you worry, baby. Home is the destination, but coming home is just the beginning of a grand adventure.

I cannot wait to explore the world with you.

XOXO
-Momma

COOPER DAY 49

April 4

Happy Easter, little bunny! I am jealous today. Jealous that little Lucas is already on room air. It is not because I am comparing you. It is because I am longing for you to come home. The level of your lung support by comparison is a heavy reminder you still have a long way to go.

This morning Jordan was searching for Easter Eggs in the backyard and all I could envision was you two searching together next year. We are painting Jordan's room soon and moving him to his big boy room, so you'll have the space-themed nursery waiting for you when you're ready.

I think about your journey home as linear. It has been anything but that. Curved, twisty, tumultuous. Sometimes the feelings and moments are hard to describe and fleeting. Today is a day my heart longs for you. For you to be home, for you to be better, for you to be whole. I love you, baby.

XO
-Momma

COOPER DAY 50

After holding you this afternoon I'm burning up. Feels like a hot flash. Between your warm cuddles, your heated vent tube on my lap and my general nervousness when I hold your fragile body, I feel like I swallowed a glass of thermogenic. Now I'm pumping: 8oz and going. I am always fuller after we cuddle. Please come home soon so you can start doing this for me.

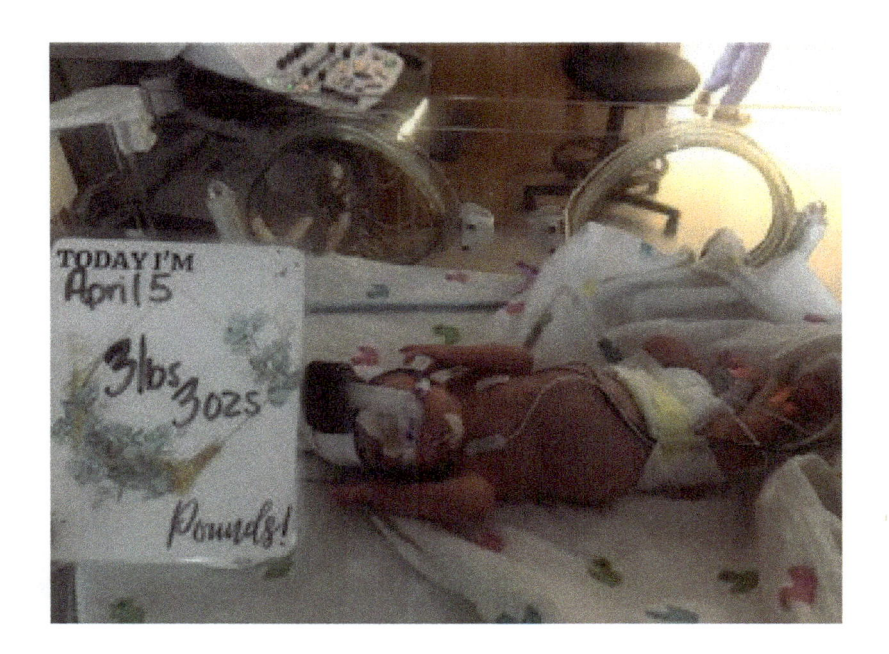

COOPER DAY 52

April 7 - 31 weeks, 6 days Gestation

"Pop a top, again!" (Lyrics from an Alan Jackson country song, look it up kid!) Your top is popped open on your isolette today for the first time, exposing your tiny body to the world as we feel it. This is excellent progress, signaling your skin is thickening and being exposed to room air won't dehydrate you. This is huge! Dad and I are SO proud.

Your FIO2 is back to 30% and no A's and B's overnight. Does not mean we are out of the woods yet, but you are doing so well.

Keep it up, baby boy!

I'm back at work for a few weeks and had lunch with clients today. All I wanted to do was talk about you.

Love you, kid.
-Mom

COOPER DAY 55

April 10

Master's Saturday!

My love for golf exploded when Dad and I met. We have always dreamed of taking family golf trips with our children. We can't wait for you to grow up and be a part of it.

Today during cuddle time we were both so warm. It's the beauty of Kangaroo Care, but also uncomfortable. You are doing great with an FIO2 in high 20's and sucking away on that pacifier. I'm so proud and love you very much. Counting down the days until we bring you home.

XOXO
-Momma

COOPER DAY 56

Eight weeks old tomorrow, baby! I came up late tonight after putting Jordan to bed and watching a new movie with Dad. I walked through the main entrance to the hospital as our old NICU neighbors from the tiny baby hallway were heading home.

They shared that their daughter has been doing well and making progress. They also shared the sad news that the tiny baby that moved into your old room was only there a short while. The baby that came after him is gone, too. We are extremely lucky, little man. You are blessed, we are blessed. And we will never forget it.

Today Hideki Matsuyama won the Masters. We had some friends over to watch. Everyone wants to meet you. I love you to the moon and back.

Forever and Always
XO
-Momma

COOPER DAY 57

Two months old today! You are scheduled to receive your two-month immunization shots this week. I met with your (yet another) Neonatologist this morning. We love having Dr. Phillips on your care, and he really has amazing faith in you going home oxygen-free given the progress you have made. What a journey! We finished a 3-dose round of Lasix, and it seemed to have done the job. No blood transfusion needed today! Your hematocrit is on the rise, which means your bone marrow is developing and you are producing red blood cells on your own! Proud of you, baby boy.

One step closer to going home.
Love,
Momma

PS: Dr. Phillips was there in the earliest days when you arrived at Texas Childrens. His point of reference on your success means quite a bit because he experienced a lot of this journey with us. At the time he was not on our care team, but now is your lead Neonatologist.

COOPER DAY 61

April 16

What a difficult, busy, but amazing week. I hate that I have not opened this journal in so long, but it may be a sign of the new ways I am beginning to process all of this. We had the Hopkins family over this week for dinner. They brought food and the whole gang. Watching their babes play together, I long for you to be home. We cannot wait for you and Jordan to have each other to play with. You are going to be best friends and that brings Dad and me so much joy. Uncle Timothy is in town and home with Jordan today. They are having a blast. I know he cannot wait to meet you. Hundreds of people cannot wait to meet you!

The nurse just came in to clear your vent tube. I walked next door to grab her a few minutes ago when I noticed all the condensation building, but I couldn't interrupt her because they were working on another critical baby. The baby is ok now, so she's come to help you. Each nurse in the unit has two babies under their assigned care at one time. Two is more than enough to keep a nurse on their feet the entire shift.

The little one next door had been crying awfully hard. I told the nurse I love baby cries here. She smiled and agreed. For babies who once were not big or strong enough to cry, it is an amazing sound that now brings peace and hope in the place of angst.

We have only just this week introduced you to social media. Many old friends and distant family members reached out to share how happy they are that you are such a fighter and offer support where they could.

It does feel good to know a greater number of people now know your name and know your story. It is a bit overwhelming.

Sitting here in your room on the family couch as you sleep, I am enjoying the calmness of this time. You have had very few alarms these past few days. The survival mode we were all in for weeks has subsided and given way to a season of waiting in peace. I am not sure how much more surviving one moment just to get to the next I could have taken. Based on your stats these recent days, we may not have to wonder. The critical season may be behind us.
XOXO,
Momma

COOPER DAY 64

MRSA (Methicillin-resistant Staphylococcus aureus)

Yesterday was a very emotional day. You tested positive for MRSA. The nurse informed us just moments after Dad and I walked into your room and were loudly cheering celebrating your new open crib. We even snapped this picture with your milestone card. The joyous moment was stolen from us.

You were moved to a crib, though! One more reason to celebrate. One less literal, physical thing standing between us. I can't wait to hold you tonight.

Love,
Momma

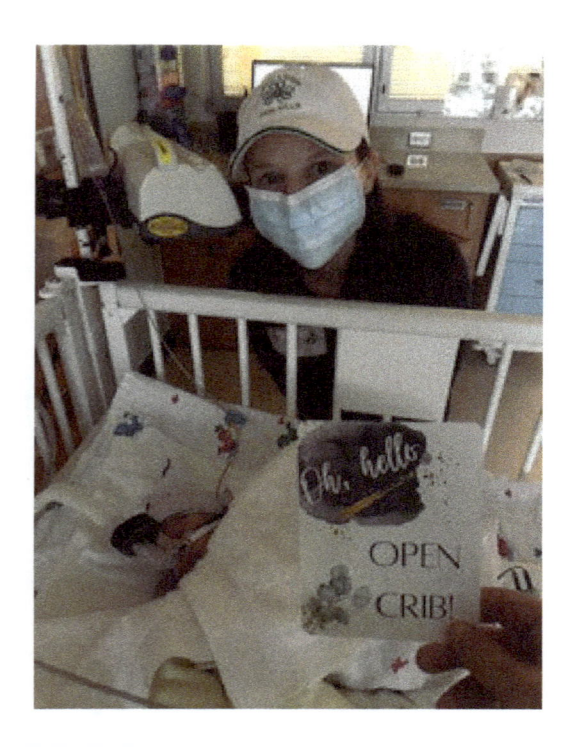

COOPER DAY 72

Hey, baby boy! Dad and I are both finally here together after a long week of stomach viruses. Last Friday we were holding you when daycare called us to pick up Jordan because he threw up during naptime. Saturday everyone was better, so Sunday Dad came up to hold you. Then I called while he was holding you because I was sick. The neighbors offered to take Jordan. Dad put you back in your crib so he could rush home to help me. I was doubled over in the front yard walking back from dropping him off. Somehow I walked back in the house, into our bathoom and laid down on the bathroom floor. Then Dad got just as sick Tuesday! We just could not win this week. Now we can finally be here with you! Since we couldn't be at the hospital with you, the weekend was spent getting the house ready for you to come home. We moved Jordan over to his new room and the nursery is ready for you! Your name is up in lights. You have a bassinet in our room ready, too. Complete with swaddles that track respiratory rate. It's going to be hard, I believe, bringing you home away from the constant monitoring. Not knowing your O2 levels every second. Your heart rate. As much as we want you home, there's comfort here.
-Momma

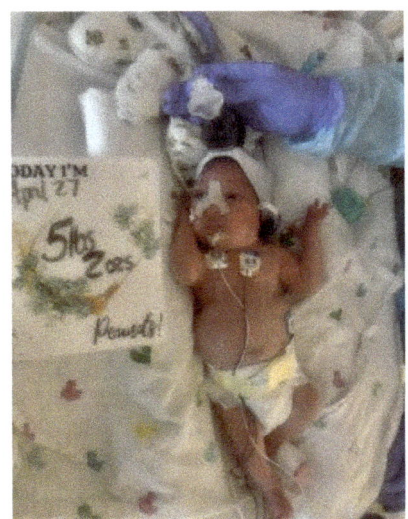

COOPER DAY 78

May 3

Last eye exam today. Way to go! No ROP! (Retinopathy of prematurity) Man, did you bellow cry during the exam, though. Another milestone in the books. Another moment that your resiliency shone through. My daydreams are filled with the moments in your life when you will have to do something hard, and you will always have this experience to look back on. Your first days are hopefully your worst days. But if they aren't, my child, I know you will still soar!

Isaiah 40:31
-Mom

COOPER DAY 80

May 5

Today you have had a ton of Brady events. These scare me. More than usual. It makes me sad to leave you today without your vitals being steady. The schedule we have settled into now runs almost like clockwork, and to stay here just 30 more minutes means my trip home will be delayed by an hour. All I can do is put on my shoes and leave like I had planned. I know you are in good hands. Headed to get brother from school now, I already miss you.

XO
-Momma

COOPER DAY 81

May 6

Hey, bud! I finally came up today. It has been since the Sunday before, and too long since I've seen you. Not by choice, just work stuff. I missed you dearly. I just held you and loved on you as much as I could. You did amazing during our hold time, too. You were down to 20.7% FIO2 and stayed there all day. When we took off your CPAP, you didn't de-sat one time. So proud of you, champ! Feels great to know you are strong. There was also talk about taking the CPAP off this Monday. We are going to discuss it with the doctors tomorrow! Mom and Dad love you so much!

Proud of you!
-Dad

COOPER DAY 82

May 7

So... May 10th is going to be a big day. We are going to remove the CPAP and see how you do. We are all so proud of you and just so blessed and blown away with your fight and progression. There is light at the end of the tunnel. Mom and Dad love you more than you'll ever know.

Beyond proud! Love you, Champ!
-Dad

COOPER DAY 83

May 8

You weigh 5lbs, 11.7oz and are finally growing very chunky rolls all over. Dad and Jordan are on their way to pick me up from the hospital. I got here early so we could cuddle, then we are taking Jordan to the zoo. Good news! You laid on your side and sucked the paci for 15 minutes while you fed.

Bad news? You spit up a short while later and your lips turned blue. Brady and de-sat to 70. My heart dropped, but it's a reminder you still need time.

I love you!
-Momma

COOPER DAY 84

April 9, Mother's Day

Dad surprised Jordan and I by booking us a night's stay at the Marriott downtown for tonight. He feels very strongly that we need to celebrate the day and take a break from hospital life. They are picking me up after our hold time at 12pm.

The weather is nice, we packed our bathing suits to swim in the rooftop pool. That pool better be heated. The thought of doing something fun with the three of us is exciting, but it does still make me sad you will miss out. There will be many staycations and Mother's Days to celebrate together. For now, I'll make the most of our time together. Damn, do we need a break. Not from you. Only from the waiting for you to come home.

Your dad is a very special man. My hope is you grow up to be like the kind husband he is to me and the loving father he is to you both.

Miss you, love! See you tomorrow afternoon!
Thanks for choosing me to be your mom.
-E

COOPER DAY 87

May 12

You latched! You latched! It was only for a second, you were frustrated, but you latched! You were alert, hungry and looking for food. So cool, baby boy! Each of your care team members said to expect big changes in the coming weeks. Between 35-37 weeks you'll become a different baby, and without CPAP you would be different, too. I stayed the night Monday night to get to know this new baby that's CPAP free and let me tell ya- you are different! Making so many grunts, noises, coos, bearing down to pass gas. Mostly gas caused by the new formula being mixed into your feedings. No more constant air pressure forced into your nose and mouth, no hot air blowing in your face. You feel calmer when I hold you. We moved your OG tube to your nose (now an NG tube) after we removed CPAP Monday. The NG tube and the leads/wires are the only things tethering you to your crib. We will be moving you back via ambulance transport to Methodist West Monday where you were born. It's bittersweet to leave Pavilion. These teams saved your life.

We will forever be grateful to them beyond words. Beyond what we can express. I'm still trying to find a way and I hope one day I can give back what I received here. What we received. You. We received you.

I promise to always pour love into you and to give more than I take.

XO
-Mom

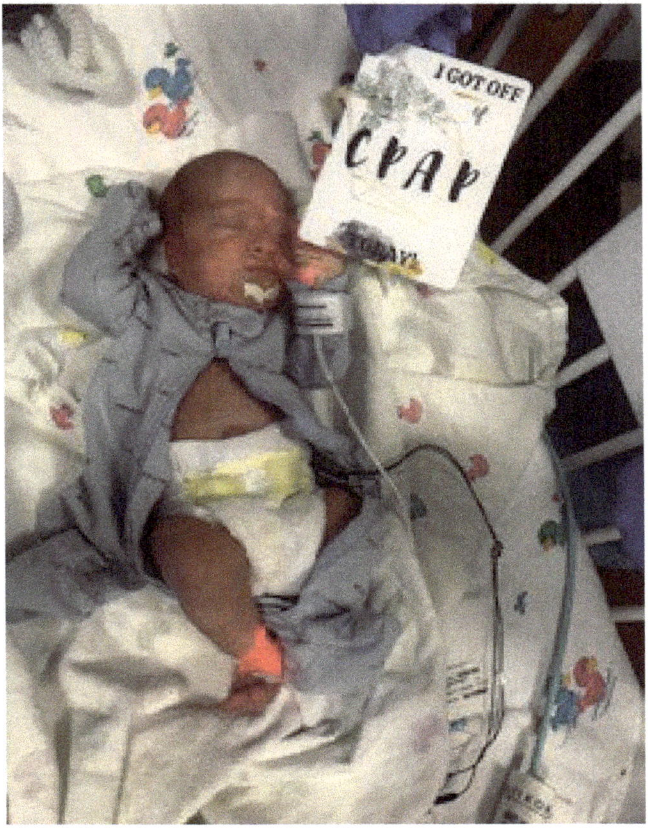
I GOT OFF
CPAP

COOPER DAY 88

May 13

Today I was able to hold you at the 9am, 12pm and 3pm feedings. You tried latching at 9am but could not commit. After that we just cuddled. We've almost made 90 days exclusively pumping, what's a few more?

I had time with your Occupational Therapist today and time with the ECI (Early Childhood Intervention) Specialist. ECI is what I intended to do with my degree after graduation. I traveled down to the Houston medical center my senior year searching for an intership. The internships are very hard to come by. ECI Specialists are the critical link connecting a long-term hospital experience with personal needs or expectations of patients and families. She gifted us two books to read with Jordan. Stories specific to being the older sibling to a NICU baby and how waiting at home can be quite hard. What a special gift! I wish we'd had these weeks ago. She is also sending us materials to learn and track milestone markers for cognitive development. I have some anxiety about not just what bringing you home looks like, but making sure we use all the resources we can to set you up for success.

Who knew I'd be anything but excited about bringing you home?
-Mom

COOPER DAY 92

May 17

I am tired. Stayed here at Pavilion with you since it is our last night here. Tears continue to well up as I walk the halls and move through our daily routine. Unexpected emotions crept up on me. The familiar faces, the steady state of the bigger baby hallway you have lived in for weeks. There is comfort here. The assured strength I have been able to lean on through this experience is found in the mundane nuances of this place. The sign on the door reminding us to wash our hands. The glowing red Texas Children's screensavers from the computers when the lights are dimmed. The beeps to which we have grown accustomed. The nurses rotate patient care but have always come back to us days or weeks later. The medicine cart making its regular rounds. The faces of the Neonatologists that had been rotated from our care. A trail of signals to my heart reminds me how much time has passed and the numerous milestones you have graduated through in our time here.

Since we are being discharged, I must take your milk home from the NICU milk bank. The best solution I could muster: our wheeled beach cooler. It's the only solution big enough to transport this volume of milk. There are ~1,000ozs in this cooler. For some reason this feels dirty to me, though I scrubbed it clean at home this morning. We've operated under such sterile conditions for three months, anything else feels gross.

I drank out of a garden hose, and I do not remember drinking from a plastic water bottle most of my childhood. Children are not as fragile as we think. Our 3-month stay in the NICU has proven that to me more than anything else.

I have an odd feeling that overwhelms my body, and it comes in waves. Mental fatigue. Though I'm rested and fed, my head feels heavy. Now that you're older I am beginning to realize how much of those first days are out of my memory. I stuffed it away until I could deal with it. Thankfully, I wrote these messages to you so we can all remember as you grow.

COOPER DAY 97

May 22

Hey, love! We moved you back to Methodist West Hospital Tuesday. The ambulance ride was a hell of a lot easier on our nerves than your first ride downtown. The smiles your progress brings to people's faces as they see you again after months away are indescribable. Many of the staff here cared for you those first five scary days, and now they lay their eyes on a five and a half pound thriving baby boy. You are really starting to get the hang of eating. I am fascinated watching you grow. One nurse mentioned you are beginning to grow out of your preemie features. I stare into your eyes and your smile searching for hints of your father and me. I see nothing familiar. You and your brother are so different in shape, scale, color and demeanor. The demeanor of a fighter, though. Could not be prouder of you. Don't tell your Dad, but that's the McCutcheon in you. Stubborn and determined.

Love,
Momma

COOPER DAY 100

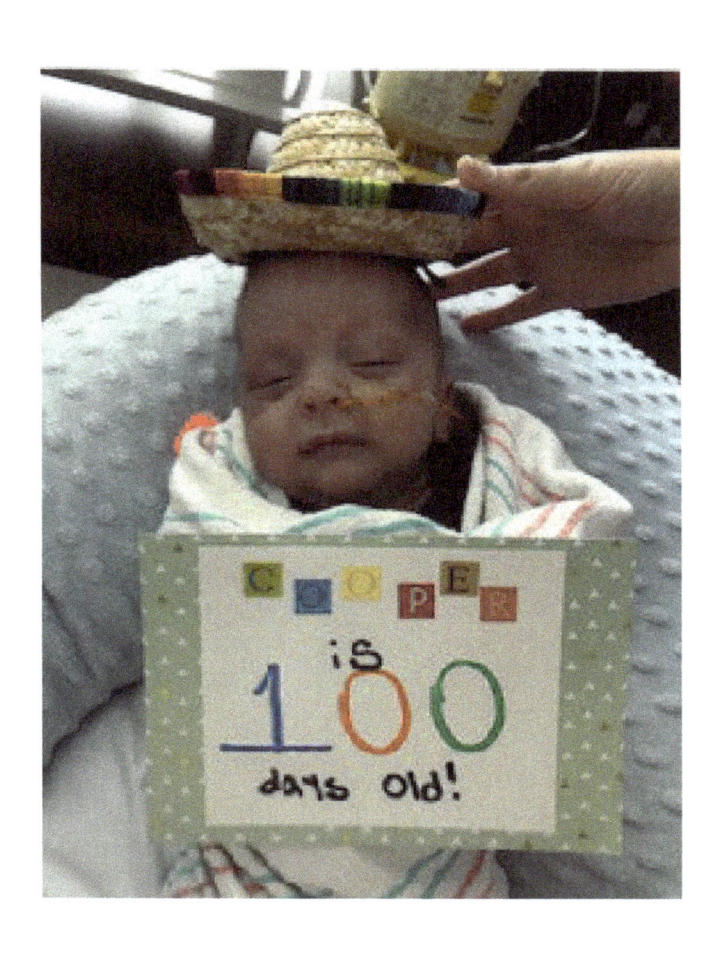

COOPER DAY 101

May 26

We were busy celebrating your 100 days yesterday and I forgot to write a journal entry. Happy 101 days, baby boy! The nurses made you a sign and took some pictures with you. Made my day! I've been quite emotional all week. My postpartum hair loss has begun, too. Such a bummer.

When someone mentions going home, I become emotional all over again. You are now taking over 80% of your bottles by mouth. 83% in the last 24 hours. As soon as you take all by mouth in 24 hours we can take the NG tube out and try another 24 hours. Then you must check a few more boxes to be cleared and you get to come home.

HOME.

Today Dad came up for your morning feed after dropping Jordan off at daycare and I stayed home to shower and feel normal. I even fixed my hair. I feel so productive once I get started, like I can change the world. The key to anything in life is starting. Momentum. Inertia.

"An object in motion remains in motion." Grandma Miller said this almost every day.

I mean, Sir Isaac Newton first, then Grandma Miller. Being productive holds different value or meaning for each of us. I hope for you a life you love, however productive or impactful. Make your life your own.
Love you!
-Momma

COOPER DAY 102

A chaplain from the hospital came by on his rounds today. He is young, or at least younger than you might expect. He asked lots of thoughtful questions. About how Dad and I had felt over the last many months. What it felt like in anticipation of taking you home. I was honest, I was slightly terrified. Ten minutes into the conversation he shared that he, too, was a preemie and after hearing your story he felt it on his heart to share. I asked him how he felt when his parents shared his NICU story with him as he grew older. I asked as I was preparing myself to one day share your story with you.

His parents did not share much at all. They did remind him how much of a miracle he was, but looking back he would have liked more detail. No one could have anticipated his journey would take him back to the NICU. We never know what lies ahead, but understanding where we have been holds power. I felt it in that moment, how glad I was we had taken the time to capture the little minutes of our journey because they can be the first ones to leave our memories.

My hope is that you find strength and comfort in this journal. That not a day in your life passes where you believe you are anything but strong and capable. A survivor.

Your biggest fan,
Mom

COOPER DAY 105

Going Home Day

On the day of your discharge home, as a parting gift to the nursing team, I brought a copy of Hoda Kotb's *I Really Needed This Today*. Her book contains anecdotal stories and words of wisdom for each day of the year. I marked and signed the page from February 20, the day your health situation became critical and required your ambulance ride to the medical center:

> **"When a flower doesn't bloom, you fix the environment, not the flower."**
> **-Alexander den Heijer**

You only needed a new environment. A new hospital. A new team and a new level of support. You were the flower.

During your doctor's morning rounds, I asked for the team to gather at your doorway. A handful of nurses and your Neonatologist paused what they were working on and gathered around your room. Many of the familiar faces had been there for your birth and your first days at Methodist. I read the February 20 entry aloud as I presented the signed book to the staff.

I cried. They cried. What a journey for all of us.

The weight of today is not heavy, but not light either. It is odd leaving. As I thought it would be. No monitors watching over you, nothing protecting you from the outside world. But you are ready.

We are ready.

The entire staff lined the NICU exit hallway, played 'Pomp and Circumstance' on a Bluetooth speaker as we left and snapped pictures of you in the cap and gown they purchased for you. We received so many hugs from some of the sweetest women I have ever met.

One special nurse escorted us out of the unit, down the elevator and through the grand lobby. A piano playing, softly. Many muffled voices in the cafeteria to the left behind us. Passing soon-to-be admitted patients walking and wheeling up to the front desk. The automatic glass doors opened as we approached. The warm spring air whooshed in and wrapped us up. With a few final, long embraces we said goodbye. We tucked you into your car seat, I climbed in the backseat with you and Dad drove our bright red truck away from under the porta cache. The sunshine hit differently. It was the first time your skin had felt the warmth of the sun.

Three stop signs in the parking lot. Three left turns and we were on our way to pick up Jordan from daycare.

We are home tonight. All four of us. Though there are tears, both yours and mine, and new routines to be found, my heart is whole.

Sweet dreams, my love. Tomorrow is just the beginning.
 -Mom

Printed in the USA
CPSIA information can be obtained
at www.ICGtesting.com
LVHW070340091024
793328LV00019B/306

9 781662 949685